iProvoke Me 99

iProvoke Me 99

KENNETH W. TAYLOR

Contents

"At some point in your life you have to fall back and look at yourself from a spectator's view. It allows you to assess your growth/ maturation in it's entirety. It also gives you an accurate measurement of your strengths and weaknesses. This creates the focus point necessary to identify the areas in your life that need the most improvement. Most importantly, falling back allows you to see the affect that you have on others. Believe it or not, each and everyone of us have a living testimony. Whether it's good or bad, we add pages to this testimony daily. With that being said, now imagine viewing yourself from the eyes of the spectator who has nothing, thirsty for a word of encouragement, and in need of definite proof that things will get better. .... What do you have to offer?"

Provoking Thoughts, Quotes, and Elaborations

1. GOD IS EVERYTHING

2. ALWAYS EXPECT YOUR BLESSINGS

3. PROSPERITY IS YOUR BIRTH RIGHT

4. THOUGHT IS THE INITIAL SPARK TO EVERY ACTION

5. "THE QUESTION ISN'T WHO'S GOING TO LET ME ... IT'S WHO'S GOING TO STOP ME" ... (AYN RAND)

6. WORDS HAVE POWER ... SPEAK YOUR MANIFESTATIONS INTO EXISTENCE

7. LIMITATIONS ARE SELF INFLICTED WOUNDS

8. THINK BIG ... SMALL THOUGHTS EQUAL SMALL RESULTS

9. ASK FOR FORGIVENESS ... NOT PERMISSION

10. "HE WHO SAYS HE CAN AND HE WHO SAYS HE CAN'T ARE USUALLY BOTH RIGHT" ... (HENRY FORD)

11. "NEGATIVITY – #1 DREAM KILLER OF ALL TIMES" ... K. TAYLOR

CAUTION: DANGEROUS VIBES!   WARNING: HIGH NEGATIVITY ALERT!

THE EFFECT THAT NEGATIVITY HAS ON A DREAM IS EQUIVALENT TO THE EFFECT THAT KRYPTONITE HAS ON SUPERMAN. NEGATIVITY CAN COME FROM MANY OUTSIDE SOURCES. UNCONSCIOUSLY EVEN OUR FAMILY, FRIENDS, AND ACQUAINTANCES ARE SOMETIMES GUILTY OF PRODUCING NEGATIVE ENERGY. BE AWARE OF THE SIGNS. IT IS A MUST THAT YOU RECOGNIZE AND DISPEL NEGATIVITY BY ANY MEANS NECESSARY. THIS IS A KEY ELEMENT TO ACHIEVING ANY GOAL THAT YOU WISH TO ACCOMPLISH.

12. "FEAR RESIDES ON THE BRIDGE TO SUCCESS" ... K. TAYLOR

13. "GOALS AND VISION KEEP YOUR LIFE COMPASS ACCURATE" ... K. TAYLOR

14. "NEVER STOP LEARNING ... MENTORS HAVE MENTORS" ... K. TAYLOR

YOU CAN NOT OBTAIN MORE THAN ENOUGH KNOWLEDGE IN ONE LIFETIME. THE WORLD IS

CONSTANTLY EVOLVING. STAY CURRENT AND ALWAYS OPEN MINDED. STAY THIRSTY!

15. "MISTAKES ARE THE CORNERSTONES OF SUCCESS" ... K. TAYLOR

MOST TESTIMONIES OF SUCCESS CONSIST OF A COUNTLESS NUMBER OF MISTAKES MADE ALONG THE WAY. DON'T ALLOW THE FEAR OF MAKING A MISTAKE TO DEFINE YOUR LIMITS. LEARN FROM YOUR MISTAKES AND KEEP BUILDING.

16. "GO INSIDE AND MEET YOUR GREATNESS" ... K. TAYLOR

SO OFTEN PEOPLE LOOK OUTWARDS FOR CONFIRMATION ABOUT THEIR RELEVANCE OR THEIR WORTH. YOUR CONFIRMATION LIES WITHIN. QUIET YOUR MIND AND LISTEN.

17. "DREAMING IS THE NEW DOING" ... K. TAYLOR

THE CONVENTIONAL WAY TO ACHIEVE A GOAL OR TO MANIFEST WHAT YOU DESIRE HAS BEEN STRICTLY BY DOING "HARD WORK". RESEARCH SHOWS THAT THE VIVID IMPRESSION OF AN IDEA IN YOUR MIND ALONG WITH THE FEELING OF BEING IN THE MIDST OF

WHATEVER IT IS YOU DESIRE IS THE MOST EFFECTIVE WAY TO MAKE A DREAM BECOME REALITY. THIS IS NOT TO SAY THAT YOU DON'T HAVE TO WORK TO REACH YOUR GOAL. ACTION MUST BE TAKEN BUT YOU SHOULD KEEP YOUR FOCUS ON THE VISION AND THE END RESULT. VISUALIZE YOURSELF CELEBRATING BECAUSE YOU HAVE ALREADY ACHIEVED YOUR GOAL. EVENTUALLY THE PARTY WILL BECOME REAL.

18. "LOVE IS THE ORIGINAL DNA OF MANKIND ... HATE IS IT'S CANCER" ... K. TAYLOR

19. "WINNERS NEVER QUIT ... LOSERS NEVER START" ... K. TAYLOR

20. "THERE IS NO BLUEPRINT FOR HAPPINESS ... SO BE CREATIVE" ... K. TAYLOR

FOLLOW YOUR OWN BLISS. WHILE IN YOUR PURSUIT OF HAPPINESS USE YOUR EMOTIONS AND FEELINGS AS INDICATORS TO LET YOU KNOW IF YOU ARE HEADED IN THE RIGHT DIRECTION. IF YOU FIND SOMETHING THAT YOU LOVE TO DO AND IT GIVES YOU GENUINE HAPPINESS, KEEP DOING THAT. FOLLOW THE FEEL GOOD PATH. IT'S USUALLY THE RIGHT ROUTE AND ALSO HAS THE LEAST RESISTANCE.

21. "NEGATIVE FEEDBACK COMES FROM THE FAN OF A LOSING TEAM" ... K. TAYLOR

22. "SUCCESS IS A VALUABLE PRODUCT OF POSITIVITY ... FAILURE IS THE PRICE YOU PAY FOR BEING NEGATIVE" ... K. TAYLOR

NEGATIVITY AND SUCCESS ARE USUALLY NOT MENTIONED IN THE SAME SENTENCE. THIS IS BECAUSE THE TWO ARE LIKE OIL AND WATER. YOU MUST CONSTANTLY STAY POSITIVE IN ORDER TO MANIFEST WHATEVER IT IS YOU DESIRE. POSITIVITY PRODUCES SUCCESS. KEEP A POSITIVE PERSPECTIVE ON YOUR GOAL AND TAKE FAILURE OFF YOUR LIST OF OPTIONS.

23. "THE EASIEST WAY TO LIFT THE BURDEN YOU CARRY IS BY HELPING SOMEONE ELSE TO LIFT THEIRS" ... K. TAYLOR

IT IS A KNOWN FACT THAT IN THE PROCESS OF HELPING SOMEONE ELSE YOUR FOCUS IS TRANSFERRED FROM SELF ONTO THE SUBJECT AT HAND. YOU LITERALLY CAN NOT HAVE FOCUS IN TWO PLACES AT ONE TIME. THEREFORE, YOUR BURDEN IS AUTOMATICALLY LIGHTENED.

24. "Raise the bar ... Test your limits ... Delve
into the unknown ... Claim what rightfully
belongs to you" ... K. Taylor

*The only way you'll know how far you can go
or how much you can accomplish is if you try
something you've never tried before. Exert
yourself past your limitations and extend
your outreach. There is an abundant amount
of blessings with your name on them simply
waiting for you to claim them.*

25. "Believe in yourself ... Stand strong on
your moral foundation ... Keep a burning
desire to accomplish your goal" ... K. Taylor

26. "Enthusiasm sparks action ... Action fires
up momentum ... Momentum lights the torch
of achievement" ... K. Taylor

27. "We are all Kings and Queens ... You just
have to accept your crown" ... K. Taylor

*Every individual possesses a greatness about
his or herself. Embrace your God given
wonderfulness and accept the rewards of
being you!*

28. "THE VICTORY DANCE FEELS MUCH BETTER WHEN YOU'RE TOO EXHAUSTED TO KEEP A BEAT" ... K. TAYLOR

29. "CHASE YOUR DREAMS AS IF THEY WERE CHASING YOU" ... K. TAYLOR

30. " LOOK FOR YOUR AWESOMENESS THROUGH THE EYES OF THE BEHOLDER ... IT WON'T BE HARD TO FIND ... IF YOU STUMBLE ACROSS GREATNESS IT SHOULD BE RIGHT NEXT TO IT" ... K. TAYLOR

31. "YOUR THOUGHTS ARE LIKE A STEERING WHEEL ... TAKE CONTROL OF THEM AND YOU WILL CRUISE TO THE DESTINATION OF YOUR CHOICE" ... K. TAYLOR

THOUGHTS CREATE YOUR REALITY. YOU HAVE LITERALLY THOUSANDS OF THOUGHTS THAT ENTER YOUR MIND DAILY. THE THOUGHTS YOU FOCUS ON AND GIVE THE MOST ATTENTION TO ARE GENERALLY WHAT YOU MANIFEST THROUGHOUT THE DAY. A PROLONGED FOCUS ON A THOUGHT WILL ULTIMATELY EFFECT YOUR ENTIRE LIFE. PICK AND CHOOSE THE THOUGHTS THAT WILL BENEFIT YOU THE MOST.

32. "KEEP YOUR FAITH IN GOD ... RELY ON HIS

GUIDANCE TO DIRECT YOU ... GIVE THANKS DAILY" ...
K. TAYLOR

33. "FAILURE AND SUCCESS HAVE ONE COMMON
BASIS ... THEY ARE BOTH PREDETERMINED
OUTCOMES" ... K. TAYLOR

*THE MOMENT YOU SET A GOAL IN YOUR MIND YOU
HAVE TWO OPTIONS. YOU CAN EITHER BELIEVE THAT
YOU WILL ACHIEVE YOUR GOAL AT ANY COST OR YOU
CAN BECOME DOUBTFUL HAVING THE FEELING THAT
IT IS ALMOST IMPOSSIBLE TO ACCOMPLISH. EITHER
ROUTE YOU TAKE THE OUTCOME HAS ALREADY BEEN
DETERMINED. THE CHOICE IS YOURS, CHOOSE
WISELY.*

34. "WHAT YOU EXPERIENCE TODAY IS A DIRECT
REFLECTION OF THE THOUGHTS YOU HAD YESTERDAY
... TODAY I AM DECLARING THAT MY THOUGHTS ARE
POSITIVE, MATURE, AND PROSPEROUS ... TOMORROW
CAN'T COME SOON ENOUGH!" ... K. TAYLOR

*LIFE IS A CONSTANT CYCLE OF CAUSE AND EFFECT.
THEREFORE IT WOULD BE TO YOUR ADVANTAGE
TO KEEP POSITIVE THOUGHTS IN YOUR MIND ABOUT
YOUR FUTURE. YOU CREATE REALITY WITH YOUR*

THOUGHTS SO CREATE YOURSELF A BETTER TOMORROW!

35. "YOU HAVE TO BE YOUR OWN #1 FAN BEFORE YOU CAN EXPECT OTHERS TO RECOGNIZE YOUR STAR QUALITIES" ... K. TAYLOR

YOU ARE THE "FEATURE PRESENTATION" AND THE CRITIC. HOW YOU RATE YOURSELF IS HOW OTHERS WILL RATE YOU. THE RECOGNITION OF YOUR OWN SELF-WORTH AND TALENT OVER A PERIOD OF TIME STARTS TO BUILD SELF-CONFIDENCE. IT EVENTUALLY BEGINS TO OVERFILL AND SPILL OUT THROUGH YOUR WORDS, ACTIONS, AND YOUR CHARACTER. YOUR WHOLE BEING WILL EXUDES GREATNESS AND LEAVE OTHERS WITH NO CHOICE BUT TO RECOGNIZE WHO YOU ARE.

36. "NURTURE YOUR DREAM LIKE A CHILD UNTIL IT DEVELOPS INTO A FULL GROWN REALITY" ... K. TAYLOR

LIKE A CHILD YOUR GOAL, DREAM, OR VISION REQUIRES YOUR FULL ATTENTION. CONSTANTLY THINK ABOUT IT, TEND TO IT, AND DO ALL OF THE THINGS NECESSARY TO HELP IT MANIFEST INTO YOUR REALITY.

37. "TAKE YOUR FAITH AND GO WINDOW SHOPPING ... KEEP YOUR FAITH AND WAIT FOR THE DELIVERY TRUCK" ... K. TAYLOR

38. "DESIGN YOUR OWN FUTURE ... DO NOT ALLOW BLIND CARPENTERS TO BUILD YOUR HOUSE AS THEY SEE FIT" ... K. TAYLOR

VIEWS AND OPINIONS ABOUT YOUR LIFE CAN COME FROM MANY OUTSIDE SOURCES. SOME OF THE INFORMATION OR ADVICE MAY BE USEFUL AND THE OTHER SIMPLY MAY NOT APPLY. SET YOUR OWN PATH IN LIFE. REMEMBER THERE ISN'T A BLUEPRINT AND THE MAP DOESN'T EXIST!

39. "DOUBTS ARE THE HECKLERS THAT ARE INSIDE OF YOU ... ESCORT THEM OUT AND RECEIVE YOUR STANDING OVATION" ... K. TAYLOR

"IF YOU HAVE FAITH AS A MUSTARD SEED, YOU WILL SAY TO THIS MOUNTAIN, MOVE FROM HERE TO THERE, AND IT WILL MOVE; AND NOTHING WILL BE IMPOSSIBLE FOR YOU" ... (MATTHEW 17:20)

ELIMINATE ALL DOUBT AND HAVE FAITH THAT YOU CAN ACHIEVE ANY GOAL THAT YOU HAVE SET IN YOUR MIND. WALK IN FAITH AND MANIFEST YOUR DREAM.

40. "WHAT YOU LOVE TO DO ... LOVES TO REWARD YOU FOR DOING IT" ... K. TAYLOR

41. "POSITIVITY IS CONTAGIOUS ... INFECT THE WORLD" ... K. TAYLOR

42. "BELIEVING IS THE NEW SEEING ... ALLOW FAITH TO PAINT YOU A MASTERPIECE" ... K. TAYLOR

IN RECENT YEARS THE SUPPRESSED KNOWLEDGE OF THE "LAW OF ATTRACTION" HAS BECOME MORE PREVALENT IN HUMAN AWARENESS. THIS IS A UNIVERSAL LAW THAT STATES "LIKE ATTRACTS LIKE". RESEARCH SHOWS THAT WE ATTRACT THINGS WITH THE THOUGHTS WE HAVE IN OUR MIND AND ALSO THAT FOCUSING ON A THOUGHT ATTRACTS IT FASTER. IT HAS ALSO BEEN FOUND OUT THAT A POSITIVE THOUGHT IS A 100 TIMES MORE POWERFUL THAN A NEGATIVE THOUGHT. MORE AND MORE PEOPLE ARE BEGINNING TO USE THIS CONCEPT TO THEIR ADVANTAGE. AS A RESULT, THE INTERNET HAS BEEN FLOODED WITH AN INCREASING NUMBER OF NEW TESTIMONIES. THINK POSITIVE, HAVE FAITH, AND CREATE A TESTIMONY OF YOUR OWN.

43. "STAND ALONE AS A LEADER OR FALL WITH THE FLOCK OF FOLLOWERS" ... K. TAYLOR

44. "TAKE A COUNT OF PERSONAL VICTORIES OVER PUBLIC LOSSES" ... K. TAYLOR

CELEBRATE ALL OF YOUR ACHIEVEMENTS, EVEN IF IT IS SOMETHING AS SMALL AS LEARNING A NEW WORD. REJOICE EVERY TIME YOU DO SOMETHING THAT GETS YOU CLOSER TO REACHING YOUR GOAL. DO NOT CONCERN YOURSELF WITH PUBLIC VIEWS OR OPINIONS. INSTEAD, STAY FOCUSED AND KEEP STRIVING FOR WHATEVER IT IS YOU DESIRE.

45. "PERCEPTION ... THE ABILITY TO SEE WEALTH IN A HOMELESS PERSON EVEN IF YOU RESIDE UNDER THE SAME BRIDGE" ... K. TAYLOR

YOUR PERCEPTION OF YOURSELF OR OF OTHERS MAY VARY DEPENDING ON THE CURRENT SITUATION. TO MAKE AN ACCURATE ASSESSMENT OF A PERSON YOU MUST DISREGARD OUTER APPEARANCE. INSTEAD YOU SHOULD EVALUATE INNER QUALITIES, TRAITS, AND CHARACTER. DO NOT ALLOW LIFE'S CURVE BALL TO DEFINE POSSIBILITY.

"YOU CAN'T JUDGE A BOOK BY IT'S COVER"

46. "GREAT MINDS DISCUSS IDEAS ... AVERAGE

MINDS DISCUSS EVENTS ... SMALL MINDS DISCUSS PEOPLE" ... (ELEANOR ROOSEVELT)

47. "LOVE LIKE GOD ... LIVE LIFE GOOD" ... K. TAYLOR

48. "CONCENTRATE YOUR FOCUS ON YOUR GOALS AND VISIONS ... DON'T ALLOW ANY NEGATIVE DISTRACTIONS TO BREAK YOUR FOCUS ... YOU WILL SOON REALIZE THAT YOU ARE IN THE MIDST OF YOUR GOALS AND VISIONS ... THEY ARE NO LONGER A FANTASY ... THEY ARE REAL AND ATTAINABLE ... YOU ARE NOW IN THE MANIFESTATION PROCESS" ... K. TAYLOR

49. "THE DEFINITION OF INSANITY IS DOING THE SAME THING OVER AND OVER AGAIN EXPECTING A DIFFERENT RESULT" ... (ALBERT EINSTEIN)

CHANGE IS ONE OF THE MOST DIFFICULT TASK IN THE WORLD TO DO. YOU DESIRE A BETTER LIFE, YET YOU FEEL THE ONLY WAY TO MAINTAIN WHAT YOU HAVE IS BY CONTINUOUSLY DOING WHAT YOU'VE BEEN DOING. THIS WAY OF THINKING WILL LEAVE YOU PARALYZED AND STUCK AT A STAND STILL. ARE YOU SATISFIED WITH WHAT YOU'RE EXPERIENCING TODAY AS A RESULT OF DOING WHAT YOU'RE

ACCUSTOM TO DOING JUST TO GET BY? IF YOU DON'T HAVE HARD EVIDENCE OF YOUR CURRENT METHOD BEING BENEFICIAL TO YOU OR TO WHAT YOU WANT TO ACCOMPLISH, STEP INTO THE UNKNOWN AND TRY SOMETHING NEW. NO NEED TO WORRY YOU'VE DONE IT YOUR WAY LONG ENOUGH TO HAVE PERFECTED IT. SO YOU CAN ALWAYS GO BACK TO "OLD FAITHFUL" IF ALL ELSE FAILS. AS FOR NOW EXPLORE OTHER OPTIONS AND EXPAND YOUR HORIZON TO SEE SOMETHING YOU'VE NEVER SEEN BEFORE. SEE NEW RESULTS. YOU HAVE NOTHING TO LOSE AND EVERYTHING TO GAIN.

50. "OBSTACLES ARE INDICATORS THAT YOU'RE HEADED IN THE RIGHT DIRECTION" ... K. TAYLOR

51. "PUSH YOURSELF UNTIL YOU ARE PULLING OTHERS ... LIFT OTHERS UNTIL THEY ARE LIFTING YOU" ... "CROWN US WE ARE ALL KINGS AND QUEENS" ... K. TAYLOR

MAKE UP YOUR MIND AND DECIDE TO BECOME A BETTER YOU. KEEP STRIVING TO IMPROVE YOUR LIFE EVEN WHEN THE JOURNEY BECOMES OVERWHELMING. REMEMBER AS QUOTE #23 STATES, "THE EASIEST WAY TO LIFT THE BURDEN YOU CARRY IS TO HELP SOMEONE ELSE TO LIFT THEIRS".

17

THE ACT OF HELPING OTHERS TO IMPROVE THEIR LIFE WILL AUTOMATICALLY ENHANCE YOUR SITUATION. IT IS OUR JOB TO MOTIVATE OTHERS AND BUILD THEM UP UNTIL THEY ARE ABLE TO RETURN THE ENCOURAGEMENT. THIS PROCESS OF EXCHANGING SUPPORT WILL HELP YOU TO ADVANCE TO HIGHER LEVELS OF IMPROVEMENT.

"AS IRON SHARPENS IRON, SO ONE PERSON SHARPENS ANOTHER" ... (PROVERBS 27:17)

52. "GOD IS MY HEAD COACH ... SO THE GAME IS ALREADY WON ONCE I ENTER THE STADIUM" ... K. TAYLOR"

53. "TALENT IS NATURAL ... SKILLS ARE DEVELOPED ... THE ABILITY TO WAKE UP EACH MORNING AND EXECUTE IS GOD GIVEN" ... K. TAYLOR

ALTHOUGH ALL OF THESE ATTRIBUTES ARE A GIFTS FROM GOD, BEING ABLE TO WAKE UP EACH MORNING GENERATES THE MOST GRATITUDE. GRATITUDE IS THE WARM AND DEEP APPRECIATION OF KINDNESS OR BENEFITS RECEIVED. THIS IS A KEY ELEMENT OF LIVING A LIFE OF FULFILLMENT.

54. "SUCCESS IS YOUR NOSY NEIGHBOR THAT'S

ALWAYS KNOCKING WHEN YOU'RE WRESTLING WITH
DOUBT AND FEAR ... TELL YOUR FAITH TO DO YOU A
FAVOR AND ANSWER THE DOOR" ... K. TAYLOR

*FAITH DIMINISHES DOUBT AND FEAR. DO NOT
CONCERN YOURSELF WITH HOW YOU'RE GOING TO
ACHIEVE YOUR GOAL. JUST KEEP YOUR FAITH AND
KNOW THAT YOU'RE GOING TO ACCOMPLISH IT.
SUCCESS IS RIGHT AROUND THE CORNER. INVITE IT
OVER!*

55. "YOUR AMBITION IS YOUR DREAM ...
UNCHAINED!" ... K. TAYLOR

56. "IDLE NEGATIVE TALK IS NO MORE THAN A
CAPTION ... SMALL WORDS UNDER THE BIG PICTURE"
... K. TAYLOR

57. "THE GREATEST DANGER FOR MOST OF US IS NOT
THAT WE AIM TOO HIGH AND WE MISS IT BUT THAT IT
IS TOO LOW AND WE REACH IT" ... (MICHELANGELO)

"DROP THE TOP ON YOUR LIMITATIONS" ... K.
TAYLOR

"NO CEILINGS" ... (LIL TUNECHI)

58. "I DESERVE PROSPERITY – GOOD THINKING ... I

WILL PROSPER – BETTER THINKING … I AM
PROSPEROUS – RIGHT THINKING!" … K. TAYLOR

59. "I GRATEFULLY HOLD THE DOOR OPEN FOR MORE
THINGS TO BE GRATEFUL FOR" … K. TAYLOR

*THE FEELING OF GRATITUDE IS AN ESSENTIAL PART
OF MANIFESTING MORE INTO YOUR
LIFE. GRATITUDE CREATES A FLOW OF ABUNDANCE
THAT INCREASES OR DECREASES DEPENDING ON HOW
GRATEFUL YOU ARE FOR THE THINGS YOU ALREADY
HAVE. THE ACT OF BEING GRATEFUL ALLOWS YOU TO
RECEIVE MORE THINGS TO BE GRATEFUL FOR.
APPRECIATE ALL OF THE THINGS YOU HAVE AND
EXPECT TO RECEIVE MUCH MORE.*

60. "LIVE IN THE FUTURE OR REPEAT THE
PRESENT"… K. TAYLOR

61. "GOD MADE US IN HIS IMAGE … THEREFORE,
THE IMAGE YOU SEE IN THE MIRROR SHOULD
REFLECT THE MOST HIGH … THE IMAGE YOU CARRY
DAILY SHOULD BE DIVINE … THERE AREN'T
ANY PERFECT HUMANS ON EARTH BUT WE SHOULD
STRIVE FOR PERFECTION … OUR CREATOR HAS SET
THE BAR FOR US … WHO ARE WE TO SETTLE FOR
ANYTHING LESS?" … K. TAYLOR

" HAVE NO FEAR OF PERFECTION ... YOU'LL NEVER REACH IT" ... (SALVADOR DALI)

ALTHOUGH "LIMITATIONS ARE SELF INFLICTED WOUNDS", THE THOUGHT THAT THERE IS A LIMIT USUALLY CAME FROM AN OUTSIDE SOURCE. IT IS COMMON FOR PEOPLE TO PROJECT THEIR OWN PERSONAL LIMITATIONS OR BELIEFS. SOME PEOPLE SEEM TO THINK THAT IT'S WRONG FOR YOU TO STRIVE FOR SOMETHING THAT ONLY THE MOST HIGH HAS. WHY SHOULDN'T PERFECTION BE THE ULTIMATE GOAL? WHO PUT A LIMIT ON HOW GOOD WE COULD BECOME? THERE IS NOTHING AVERAGE ABOUT GOD, ESPECIALLY NOT HIS IMAGE!

62. "THOSE WHO RECEIVE ABUNDANTLY HAVE TRULY MASTERED THE ART OF GIVING" ... K. TAYLOR

THE LAW OF GIVING AND RECEIVING IS A UNIVERSAL LAW. THE MORE YOU GIVE THE MORE YOU WILL RECEIVE. THE CYCLE IS CONSTANTLY FLOWING.

63. "POSITIVE OR NEGATIVE ... AWARE OR UNAWARE ... CARE OR DON'T CARE ... YOUR THOUGHTS CREATE YOUR REALITY" ... K. TAYLOR

64. "SPEND YOUR PASTIME ... MAKING YOUR FUTURE ... BECOME YOUR PRESENT" ... K. TAYLOR

SACRIFICE – A SURRENDER OF SOMETHING OF VALUE AS A MEANS OF GAINING SOMETHING MORE DESIRABLE

GIVE UP SOME OF YOUR LEISURE TIME AND FOCUS ON CREATING YOUR FUTURE. INSTEAD OF HANGING OUT, WORK ON A GOAL WITH INTENSITY. USE YOUR DAYDREAMING TIME TO YOUR ADVANTAGE AND VISUALIZE YOURSELF IN THE MIDST OF THE LIFESTYLE YOU DESIRE. EVENTUALLY YOU WILL MANIFEST WHATEVER YOU DESIRE INTO YOUR REALITY.

65. "NO MORE DREAMING AND CONTEMPLATION ... TIME FOR ACTION AND COMPENSATION ... BECOME ONE WITH THE SOURCE OF MANIFESTATION" ... K. TAYLOR

66. "IF KNOWLEDGE IS POWER ... I WANT TO ACQUIRE ENOUGH TO DIM THE MOON" ... K. TAYLOR

67. "YOUR VISION IS YOUR COMPASS ... GOD IS YOUR FUEL ... AND YOU ARE THE LATEST MODEL

VEHICLE WAITING TO PROVE THE SPEEDOMETER
WRONG" ... K. TAYLOR

68. "THE IMAGE YOU CARRY ON THE OUTSIDE IS A
DIRECT REFLECTION OF THE IMAGE YOU HOLD ON
THE INSIDE" ... K. TAYLOR

*A PHYSICALLY FIT PERSON CAN NOT HIDE THE FACT
THAT HE OR SHE WORKS OUT REGULARLY. THEIR
MUSCLES SIMPLY WILL NOT ALLOW IT. THE SAME IS
TRUE FOR THE THOUGHTS THAT YOU FOCUS ON IN
YOUR MIND DAILY. YOUR THOUGHTS WILL
EVENTUALLY MANIFEST AND BECOME A PART OF
YOUR OUTER IMAGE.*

69. "SPEND TIME PREPARING FOR THE PERFECT
OPPORTUNITY ... DON'T WASTE AN OPPORTUNITY
PREPARING FOR THE PERFECT TIME" ... K. TAYLOR

70."GIVE IN TO YOUR PASSION ... GIVE UP YOUR
PRIDE ... GIVE IT OVER TO GOD" ... K. TAYLOR

*CONSTANTLY DO WHATEVER GIVES YOU 100% PURE
SATISFACTION WHEN YOUR INVOLVED IN IT. GET OUT
OF YOUR OWN WAY. WALK IN FAITH AND ALLOW GOD
TO GUIDE YOU TO A WONDERFUL LIFE.*

23

71. "OUR DEEPEST FEAR IS NOT THAT WE ARE INADEQUATE ... OUR DEEPEST FEAR IS THAT WE ARE POWERFUL BEYOND MEASURE" ... (NELSON MANDELA)

"CROWN US WE ARE ALL KINGS AND QUEENS" ... K. TAYLOR

72. "SHAKE UP YOUR COMFORT ZONE WITH A GOAL AND AMBITION" ... K. TAYLOR

73. "MY MIND IS MY WEAPON ... THE AMMUNITION I CHOOSE TO FILL IT WITH DAILY IS POSITIVE THINKING WITH AN EXTRA CLIP OF BELIEF TO INSURE NO BACKFIRING" ... K. TAYLOR

"NO WEAPON FORMED AGAINST ME SHALL PROSPER" ... (ISAIAH 54:17)

SOMETIMES THE ENEMY LIES WITHIN. THIS IS DUE TO THE THOUGHTS YOU FOCUS ON THAT PARALYZE YOUR MIND. DECIDE TODAY TO AVOID NEGATIVE THINKING AND DISBELIEF IN YOURSELF. IT WILL INCREASE YOUR CHANCES OF HITTING YOUR TARGET.

74. "YOUR CONFIDENCE IS YOUR COMPETENCE MIRRORED" ... K. TAYLOR

YOUR KNOWLEDGE OF YOURSELF OR OF ANY SUBJECT MATTER DETERMINES THE AMOUNT OF CONFIDENCE THAT YOU WILL HAVE AND DISPLAY. STRIVE TO OBTAIN AS MUCH KNOWLEDGE AS YOU CAN ACQUIRE. RAISE YOUR LEVEL OF CONFIDENCE AS HIGH AS THE SKY.

75. "INCINERATE DOUBT AND FEAR WITH A BURNING DESIRE TO SUCCEED" ... K. TAYLOR

76. "THE WORLD IS AWAITING THE ARRIVAL OF YOUR VISION AND GOD HAS LAID THE RED CARPET OUT FOR YOU" ... K. TAYLOR

77. "FAITH IS THE REALITY OF WHAT WE HOPE FOR ... THE PROOF OF WHAT WE DON'T SEE" ... (HEBREWS 11:1)

78. "AN IDEA WITH INTENT IS THE SEED YOU PLANT INSIDE YOUR MIND ... BELIEF, ACTION, AND FAITH ARE THE RESOURCES USED TO CULTIVATE IT UNTIL IT BECOMES REALITY" ... K. TAYLOR

79. "DON'T FOCUS ON YOUR SCORE WITH COMPETITION ... FOCUS ON YOUR CORE WITH COMPETENCE" ... K. TAYLOR

Do not concern yourself with what others are doing. Do not mentally compare your progress or accomplishments with an outside source. Instead, focus on yourself. Make sure that you constantly sharpen your skills and obtain knowledge daily. This will give you a keen sense of certainty about the task at hand and about yourself. Keep building a better you until the competition's score is irrelevant.

80. "Perception ... The ability to be the main event if you are first to go on stage ... Also the ability to know that the acts before you are merely openers if you're last to go on" ...
K. Taylor

Your perception defines and shapes your reality. Do not allow others to have an influence on how you perceive a situation in your life. Instead, internalize and evaluate the situation. Perceive a single encounter in the way that benefits you the most.

81. We are all self-made ... but only the successful will admit it ... (Earl Nightingale)

82. "IN LIFE THERE ARE LESSONS THAT YOU MUST LEARN BEFORE YOU CAN ADVANCE ... SOUL SEARCH AND DISCOVER THE SOURCE OF YOUR ROADBLOCK" ... K. TAYLOR

IT IS IN OUR HUMAN NATURE TO ADVANCE AND IMPROVE. AT BIRTH WE BEGAN OUR JOURNEY IN SEARCH OF "BETTER". WHETHER IT'S A BETTER TOY, A BETTER CAR, A BETTER UNDERSTANDING, A BETTER RELATIONSHIP, OR A BETTER LIFE WE ARE NATURALLY INCLINED TO ASPIRE FOR MORE. IF YOU FIND YOURSELF STUCK AND UNABLE TO ADVANCE, SEARCH INWARD FOR THE CAUSE. IN MOST CASES THERE'S SOMETHING MINOR HOLDING YOU BACK FROM SOMETHING MAJOR.

83. "THE REASON THERE ISN'T ANY CHANGE IN YOUR LIFE IS BECAUSE YOU ARE LOOKING FOR CHANGE ... YOU HAVE TO BECOME THE CHANGE ... EVENTUALLY THE CHANGE WILL BECOME YOUR REALITY" ... K. TAYLOR

84. "WE CAN ALL SPECTATE THE PLOT OF THE DIVINE ... YOU JUST HAVE TO DESIGNATE THE THOUGHTS IN YOUR MIND ... PREPARE TO DEDICATE A LOT OF YOUR TIME ... AND DON'T HESITATE OR YOU'LL LOSE YOUR SPOT IN LINE" ... K. TAYLOR

27

MAKE IT CLEAR IN YOUR MIND ABOUT WHAT YOU WISH TO OBTAIN, ACCOMPLISH, OR ACHIEVE. PUT IN THE WORK AND TIME THAT IS NEEDED TO MAKE IT HAPPEN. STAY DILIGENT AND TAKE ACTION WHEN IT'S TIME TO TAKE ACTION! MOVE OUT OF THE WAY AND EXPECT IT TO MANIFEST. IT'S JUST THAT SIMPLE!

85. "OPEN YOUR MIND TO INCREASE YOUR VISION ... OPEN YOUR HEART TO INCREASE YOUR BLESSING" ... K. TAYLOR

86. "LET GOD BE YOUR DESIGNATED DRIVER ... HE GUARANTEES YOU'LL GET THERE SAFE AND ON TIME ... NO CHARGE" ... K. TAYLOR

87. "THE DEFINITION OF SANITY IS DOING THE RIGHT THING OVER AND OVER WITH INTENT ... FULLY EXPECTING THE BEST RESULTS" ... K. TAYLOR

88. "TIME IS ABUNDANT FOR THE WATCHER ... SCARCE FOR THE DOER ... AND A NON-FACTOR FOR THE BELIEVER" ... K. TAYLOR

A PERSON WHO MERELY OBSERVES ANOTHER PERSON'S MANIFESTATIONS USUALLY HAS PLENTY OF TIME TO TAKE COUNT OF ALL THE BLESSING BEING RECEIVED AROUND THEM. THE INDIVIDUAL WHO

BELIEVES THERE IS SOMETHING THAT HAS TO BE DONE AT ALL TIMES IN ORDER TO MANIFEST HARDLY HAS TIME FOR ANYTHING. AS FOR THE PEOPLE WHO BELIEVE THAT THEY CAN AND WILL MANIFEST WHAT THEY DESIRE, TIME SEEMS TO STAND STILL.

89. "YOU ARE DESIGNED TO BE AN ARTIST ... SEARCH FOR YOUR CANVAS AND DISPLAY YOUR GOD GIVEN TALENTS" ... K. TAYLOR

EACH AND EVERY INDIVIDUAL HAS A TALENT, A PURPOSE, OR A GIFT TO SHARE. YOU HAVE TO FIND YOUR STAGE AND SHOW THE WORLD WHAT GOD HAS INSTALLED IN YOU.

90. "OTHERS GIVE YOU GOOD ADVICE ... YOU GIVE YOURSELF THE BEST ADVICE ... THE ANSWER LIES WITHIN ... QUIET YOUR MIND AND LISTEN" ... K. TAYLOR

91. "YOUR GOAL AND YOUR LIMIT ARE USUALLY RIGHT NEXT TO EACH OTHER ... KEEP REACHING" ... K. TAYLOR

92. "CHANGE YOUR PERCEPTION ... IMPOSSIBLE, I'M

POSSIBLE, I AM POSSIBLE, I AM ALL POSSIBILITY" ...
K. TAYLOR

93. "LIFE ... LEARNED ILLUSTRATIONS FACILITATING EVERYONE" ... K. TAYLOR

THIS WHOLE CONCEPT CALLED LIFE IS A SERIES OF EVENTS AND LESSONS THAT YOU ARE A WITNESS TO. LIFE GIVES YOU A NEW SCENARIO DAILY FILLED WITH LESSONS THAT YOU CAN LEARN FROM. THE ACQUISITION OF KNOWLEDGE IS ESSENTIAL TO LIVING A LIFE OF FULFILLMENT. WHAT YOU CHOOSE TO BELIEVE, OBTAIN, AND UTILIZE WILL SHAPE HOW YOU LIVE YOUR LIFE.

94. "A SUCCESSFUL LIFE WILL COST YOU ONE DREAM ... BUT THE DREAM IS FREE" ... K. TAYLOR

95. "IF YOU'RE THINKING "I WANT" CHANCES ARE YOU WILL NEVER HAVE ... IF YOU'RE THINKING "I HAVE" CHANCES ARE YOU WILL NEVER WANT" ... K. TAYLOR

96. "LIFE HAS LEVELS WITHOUT LIMITATIONS ... DEATH HAS BEEN DETAINED WITHOUT DUE DATES ... LIVE YOUR LIFE TO THE FULLEST" ... K. TAYLOR

97. "THOUGHT IS THE KEY THAT OPENS THE VAULT FILLED WITH UNLIMITED GIFTS FROM GOD" ... K. TAYLOR

98. "THE PROCESS OF MANIFESTATION IS CLEARLY INVISIBLE ... A PROCESSED MANIFESTATION IS VISIBLY CLEAR" ... K. TAYLOR

DURING THE MANIFESTATION PROCESS IT IS IMPOSSIBLE TO KNOW HOW YOU WILL ACHIEVE YOUR GOAL. THEREFORE, YOU NEED NOT BURDEN YOURSELF WITH THIS DILEMMA. YOUR MAIN FOCUS SHOULD BE ON THE END RESULT. BELIEVE THAT YOU CAN ACHIEVE YOUR GOAL AND IT WILL EVENTUALLY BECOME YOUR REALITY. YOU WILL NOW BE ABLE TO LOOK BACK AT THE SERIES OF EVENTS THAT HAD TO HAPPEN IN ORDER FOR YOU TO BE WHERE YOU'RE AT NOW. EACH EVENT WILL SEEM OBVIOUS AT THIS POINT BUT NEVER IN A MILLION YEARS WOULD YOU HAVE BEEN ABLE TO KNOW THAT IT WOULD HAPPEN LIKE THIS.

99. "A TOAST TO MY FAILURES ... WITHOUT THEM I WOULDN'T BE ABLE TO HIGH-FIVE MY SUCCESS" ... K. TAYLOR

AM I INADEQUATE, ADEQUATE, OR TOO ADEQUATE?

THIS IS A COMMON QUESTION THAT OFTEN GOES UNANSWERED. LIFE ISSUES YOU A SERIES OF EVENTS THAT TEST YOUR ADEQUACY DAILY. THE MAJORITY OF THE TEST IS MENTAL AND THE REST IS A TEST OF COMPETENCY. RESEARCH SHOWS THAT YOUR PARADIGM DECIDES THE RESULT OF THE TEST. PARADIGMS ARE THE THOUGHTS AND BELIEFS THAT YOU HAVE EMBEDDED INTO YOUR SUBCONSCIOUS. THESE BELIEFS ARE HEAVILY INFLUENCED BY YOUR UP-BRINGING AND SOCIAL ENVIRONMENT. YOUR PARADIGM LITERALLY SHAPES THE REALITY THAT YOU ARE EXPERIENCING. THIS MEANS REGARDLESS OF WHETHER YOU KNOW IT OR NOT, YOUR PAST HAS AN INFLUENCE ON YOUR PRESENT AND COULD POTENTIALLY INFLUENCE YOUR FUTURE. RESEARCH ALSO REVEALS THAT POSITIVE THINKING, BELIEF, AND FAITH CAN CHANGE YOUR PARADIGM. NEVER HAVE FEAR OF BEING INADEQUATE. YOU MUST REMEMBER THAT NO ONE HAS A BLUEPRINT TO THIS THING CALLED LIFE. BEING ADEQUATE IS A

METAPHYSICAL STATE OF MIND. THIS MEANS THAT
ADEQUACY IS MOSTLY MENTAL AND YOU'RE THE ONLY
PERSON WHO CAN ULTIMATELY DECIDE IF YOU'RE
ADEQUATE. LAST BUT NOT LEAST, THERE IS NO SUCH
THING AS BEING TOO ADEQUATE. OBTAIN AS MUCH
KNOWLEDGE AS YOU CAN POSSIBLY ACQUIRE IN YOUR
LIFETIME. DO NOT PUT A LIMIT ON HOW GREAT YOU
CAN BECOME. STRIVE FOR PERFECTION. YOU CAN
RECEIVE ALL OF THE BLESSINGS GOD HAS FOR YOU
IF YOU SIMPLY BELIEVE THAT IT'S
POSSIBLE AND THAT YOU DESERVE IT .

CROWN US ... WE ARE ALL KINGS AND QUEENS

COMING SOON!!!

www.ingramcontent.com/pod-product-compliance
Lightning Source LLC
Chambersburg PA
CBHW041759040426
42447CB00001B/23